James Stevenson

The War of 1812

In connection with the Army Bill Act

James Stevenson

The War of 1812
In connection with the Army Bill Act

ISBN/EAN: 9783337013035

Printed in Europe, USA, Canada, Australia, Japan

Cover: Foto ©ninafisch / pixelio.de

More available books at **www.hansebooks.com**

THE

WAR OF 1812

'IN CONNECTION WITH

THE ARMY BILL ACT

BY

JAMES STEVENSON

GENERAL MANAGER OF THE QUEBEC BANK

MONTREAL

W. FOSTER BROWN & CO., PUBLISHERS

1892.

PREFACE.

Some years ago I delivered a Lecture before *The Literary and Historical Society* of Quebec, on THE CURRENCY OF CANADA AFTER THE CAPITULATION, which was published, and copies were sent to my friends. I closed my lecture with a promise to proceed with the subject. "We have now reached," I said, "the most interesting part of our financial History, that which is related to the War of 1812, when our Militia and our monetary resources were taxed to the utmost. I shall leave it to others to deal with the incidents of war : it will be my endeavour to show how the exigencies of the Army were provided for, under circumstances particularly trying, by the establishment of a Government BANK OF ISSUE, which all our writers upon the History of Canada have alluded to; but which few, if any, have described in its operations, from its inception to its close, on the return of peace." Having been frequently reminded of my promise by brother Bankers, and by several friends, I have considered it my duty to redeem my pledge—hence the following pages.

JAMES STEVENSON.

QUEBEC,
14th March, 1892.

CONTENTS.

CHAPTER I.

CHAPTER II.

CHAPTER III.

THE
CIRCULATION OF THE ARMY BILLS

WITH SOME

REMARKS UPON THE WAR OF 1812.

CHAPTER I.

Declaration of War—Embargo on Goods—Meeting of Provincial Parliament—Introduction of the Act—Legal tender coins—Capture of Detroit—Death of General Brock.

The American declaration of war was received in Quebec on Monday, the 29th June, 1812. On the 30th, a proclamation was issued by His Excellency Sir George Prevost, requiring all American citizens to depart from the Province within fourteen days ; and, by order of police, within seven days from the city and district of Quebec. Great activity prevailed in the city in putting into operation the means of defence at the immediate disposal of the government, which consisted of the ordinary peace establishment of the British troops in the Province and the colonial forces.

A militia general order was issued by the Adjutant-General, F. Vassal de Monviel, from the headquarters in Montreal on the 6th July, ordering the battalions of militia throughout the Province to hold themselves in readiness to be embodied, and to march on the shortest notice to such points as the safety of the Province might require. In Quebec the militia of the city mounted guard in company with the regular troops, and each battalion continued to furnish a proportion of its number daily for garrison duty. The flank companies belonging to the militia battalions of Montreal, were formed into a battalion under Lieut.-Col. Auldjo and Lieut.-Col. Guy. A proclamation was issued by General Isaac Brock, Governor of Upper Canada, from his headquarters, Fort George, on the 22nd July, announcing the invasion of the Province by the Americans, with the intention, he said, of conquering Canada and restoring it to the Empire of France. "Are you prepared," he said, "inhabitants of Canada, to become willing subjects, or rather slaves to the despot who rules the nations of Europe with a rod of iron,—if not, arise," etc.

On the 16th July, a temporary embargo was laid upon all goods, wares, moneys, merchandise and commodities in and within the Province of Lower Canada; upon all arms and ammunition; upon scalping knives, daggers and Indian lances, bullion and specie of every description, none of which were allowed to be exported from any port within the Province of Lower Canada. All vessels were prohibited from sailing, save such as were actually loaded or loading, and which were bound for any port in the United Kingdom, or any of the colonies in America or the West Indies. The Provincial Parliament met on the same day, and His Excellency Sir George Prevost alluded in his speech to the fruitless endeavours of His Majesty for the preservation of peace ; to his implicit confidence in the loyalty of his subjects ; to their attachment to his person ; and to their ardent love for the true interests of their country. He observed with concern that the necessary establishments of the militia forces and the operations of the approaching campaign, would be attended with considerable expense ; but he relied implicitly upon their wisdom and public spirit for such supplies as the circumstances and exigencies of the affairs of the Province would be found to require.

Loyal responses were made by the Legislative Council and House of Assembly on the 18th, the latter expressing itself prepared to grant such supplies as the exigencies of affairs might require.

The people and authorities of Canada had for a long time been alive to the imminence of war ; but at the time of the declaration of war, Canada was in a comparatively defenceless state. To man the fortresses of Quebec and Kingston, and to cover a frontier of 1,700 miles in length, the whole available force consisted of 4,450 regulars of all arms. In the Upper Province, which presents a war frontier of 1,300 miles, there were about 1,450 soldiers. The militia consisted of about 2,000 men in the Lower, and 1,800 in the Upper Province. The total population of Upper Canada at this time was under 100,000, while that of the Lower Province did not exceed 300,000.

On Sunday, the 19th July, orders for the whole of the militia of the Province to hold themselves in readiness to be embodied, was read on the Esplanade of the city of Quebec to the militiamen under arms. His Excellency was present on the occasion, and expressed his approbation of the zeal shown by the men in voluntarily doing duty with His Majesty's regular forces.

To meet the pecuniary exigencies of the war the Provincial Parliament of Lower Canada, which assembled on the 16th July, 1812, and remained in session till the 1st of August, being the third session of the seventh Parliament holden in Quebec, passed the Act to facilitate the circulation of army bills, which provided as follows :

First. That His Excellency the Governor, as Commander of His Majesty's forces, from time to time should cause to be prepared and made any number of bills, to be denominated army bills, containing one common sum, or different sums, in the principal moneys, not to exceed two hundred and fifty thousand pounds currency. Second. That such bills should be issued from an office to be called the "army bill office." Third. That the said army bills of twenty-five dollars each and upwards should bear interest at the rate of fourpence per centum per diem, upon or in respect of the several amounts of each. Fourth. That the principal sums of the said army bills of twenty-five dollars each and upwards should, at the option of the Commander of the forces, be payable on demand to the holders of such army bills, in cash or in Government bills of exchange on London, at thirty days' sight at the current rate of exchange. Fifth. That the interest of all such army bills of twenty-five dollars each and upwards, upon the payment thereof in cash or in bills of exchange as aforesaid, should be paid in army bills or in cash at the army bill office, at the option of the holders of such army bills. Sixth. That the principal sums of all such army bills of twenty-five dollars each and upwards, if paid in cash, should be paid at the army bill office; but if paid in government bills of exchange, should be paid at the office of the Commissary-General, upon a deposit in army bills of the amount of the bills of exchange to be so paid, and a certificate of such deposit under the hand and seal of the superintendent of the army bill office to the Commissary-General. Seventh. That it will be advisable for His Excellency the Commander of the forces, from time to time to cause to be prepared and made, such number of army bills of the value of four dollars each as he shall see fit, provided the said army bills of four dollars each and the said army bills of twenty-five dollars each and upwards do not together exceed the aforesaid sum of two hundred and fifty thousand pounds currency. Eighth. That the said army bills of four dollars each should be payable at the Army bill office in cash, to the bearer on demand. Ninth. That all army bills whatever should be issued as cash, upon the warrants of His Excellency as Commander of the Forces, to such person or persons, as he by such warrants shall see fit to direct such payments to be made. Tenth. That the current rate of exchange should be established on oath once in every fortnight by five persons, to be named by His Excellency, and publicly notified before any army bills whatever shall be issued. Eleventh. Makes provision for the cancellation of defaced army bills, and the reissue of new army bills of same number, tenor and date as those cancelled. Twelfth. That no army bills should be re-issued, those of four dollars each excepted, and that all army bills whatever should at all times be redeemable by being called in and paid, both principal and interest in cash. And whereas His Excellency hath been pleased to prepare and cause to be prepared such army bills to the value of two hundred and fifty thousand pounds currency, which from time to time, as required, will be issued. And whereas it is the bounden duty of the Legislature to furnish every possible aid and assistance towards the defence of the Province, and to this end it is necessary to facilitate and support the circulation of all such army bills, be it enacted that the Governor, Lieut.-Governor or person administering, the Government be authorized and empowered to pay and allow or cause to be paid out of all moneys, customs, taxes and revenues of the Province, and in preference to all other claims and demands whatsoever, all such interest at the rate of four pence per hundred pounds per diem as shall have arisen and grown due upon all every and any such army bill which shall be so issued as aforesaid, not exceeding in the whole, the sum of fifteen thousand pounds currency per annum, which said interest shall run from the day of the date of such bill or bills, and such other charges as shall be necessarily incurred in, to or for the issuing, circulating or cancelling of the said army bills, not exceeding in the whole, two thousand five hundred pounds currency per annum.

SECTION II. Provides that whatever moneys shall be issued out of the aforesaid moneys, customs, &c., shall be replaced out of the first supplies granted in the Provincial Parliament.

III. Provides that the army bills shall be current in the revenue, and taken by all collectors, and receivers in the province, and that the same in the hands of such collectors and receivers, and in the hands of the Receiver-General shall be deemed as cash.

IV. Provides that in payments to the revenue, interest shall be allowed to the day of payment, i.e., that the interest which from time to time shall be due upon any such army bill, shall be allowed to all persons, &c., paying the same to the Receiver-General or any collector or receiver up to the respective days whereupon such bill or bills shall be so paid ; Provided always that every such Receiver-

General, collectors and receivers as aforesaid, shall be accountable for the interest on every such bill, so by them or either of them received for and during which such bill shall remain in their hands.

V. Provides that all interest upon such army bills shall cease from and after the fourteenth day next after the day on which the same by any proclamation shall be called in to be redeemed in cash, and that money shall be reserved in hand for discharging the same.

VI. Sets forth the penalty on forging army bills.

VII. Enacts that all contracts shall be void in which any distinction shall be made between army bills and cash.

VIII. No arrest if a tender in army bills be made.

IX. No attachment shall issue if a deposit in Army Bills be made within the time limited by order of court.

X. On *capias ad satisfaciendum* a deposit of the debt and costs in Army Bills shall stay proceedings.

XI. On *fieri facias*, &c., a deposit of the debt and costs in army bills shall stay proceedings.

XII. Provides relief for bills destroyed or lost in case of satisfactory proof of such destruction or loss being given, together with security for payment if the bill or bills certified to be lost, burnt or destroyed, shall be thereafter produced.

XIII. Provides Provincial security for ultimate payment of army bills and loans in the following terms: And whereas there may be many persons desirous of coming forward in aid of His Majesty's Government, with the loan of monies, who, having no commercial concern whereby to dispose of bills of exchange, and who, on that account may be deterred therefrom, for remedy thereof; be it enacted that from and after the expiration of five years after the passing of this Act, each and every the holder of any and every such army bill as may remain unpaid and unsatisfied shall be entitled to receive out of and from the monies that then may be in the hands of the Receiver-General of the Province, or from the first monies that may thereafter come into his hands arising out of any taxes or duties heretofore imposed or that may hereafter be imposed, levied or raised by virtue of any Act or Acts of the Provincial legislature, or from the rents and revenues of His Majesty's territorial domains in this Province, the full amount of all such army bills in money, with the interest remaining due thereon.

XIV. Refers to the duty of the Receiver-General on the receipt and payment of army bills, viz., that he shall pay over the same to the Commissary-General for the time being and get from him the amount thereof in Government bills of exchange, at the current rate of exchange, or in cash at the option of the said Commissary-General, and the Receiver-General shall immediately thereafter render a true and exact account of all such payments and receipts to the Governor, in order that the same may be laid before the House of Assembly at the next session thereafter.

XV. And be it further enacted by the authority aforesaid, that for and during the period of five years from the passing of this Act, no person whatever shall export or otherwise carry out of this province, any gold, silver, or copper coin of any description whatsoever, or any molten gold or silver in any shape or shapes whatever, and if any person whatever shall export or otherwise carry out of this province, or procure to be exported or otherwise carry out of this province, or shall in any manner or way whatsoever, attempt or endeavour to export or otherwise carry out of this province, or attempt or endeavour to procure to be exported or otherwise carried out of this province, any gold, silver or copper coin of any description whatever, or any molten gold or silver in any shape or shapes whatever, then, in each and every such case, such gold, silver and copper coin, and such molten gold and silver shall be forfeited, one half to His Majesty, his heirs and successors, and one half to the person who shall sue for the same, and the same shall and may be seized, sued for, prosecuted, condemned and recovered in such courts, and by such and the like ways, means and methods, and the produce thereof disposed of and applied in such and the like manner, and to such and the like uses and purposes as any forfeiture incurred by any law respecting the revenue of the Customs may now be seized, sued for, prosecuted, condemned or recovered, disposed of or applied.

XVI. Refers to action against the exporter of

specie or bullion as follows : And be it further enacted that every person whatever, who, during the period of five years from the passing of this Act shall export or otherwise carry out of this province, or procure to be exported or otherwise carried out of this province, or shall put on board of any ship, or vessel, or boat, or into any land carriage to be exported or otherwise caried out of this province, or shall in any manner or way whatsoever attempt or endeavour to export or otherwise carry out of this province, or attempt or endeavour to procure to be exported any gold, silver, or copper coin of any description whatever, or any molten gold or silver, in any shape or shapes whatever, for every such offence over and above the forfeiture of such gold, silver and copper coin, and if such molten gold or silver, if the same shall be seized, shall forfeit the sum of two hundred pounds, and double the value of such gold, silver and copper coin, and of such molten gold and silver, one half to His Majesty, and one half to the person who shall sue for the same by bill, suit, action or information, in any of His Majesty's courts in this Province.

XVII. Provides that nothing in the Act shall prevent persons taking out of the Province the sum of £10, or such further sum with license from the Governor.

XVIII. Penalty on persons convicted of perjury.

XIX. Refers to fines, &c., to be paid into the hands

B

of the Receiver-General and to be accounted for to the Crown.

XX. Refers to limitations of action. At the close of the session, on the 1st of August, 1812, the Provincial Parliament of Lower Canada presented to His Excellency Sir George Prevost, Baronet, the foregoing "Act to facilitate the circulation of army bills" for the royal assent, which was duly given. The Honorable Speaker of the Assembly said: "They, the representatives of the Province of Lower Canada, are under the greatest obligation to your Excellency for having communicated to them the means to ameliorate and insure for several years the punctual payment of the army, by the circulation of bills, the reimbursement of which is guaranteed in England. To give them greater credit, this bill limits the sum necessary, and moreover provides for the interest, the advantages accruing therefrom, and for the entire payment of the principal in specie in this Province, which has become expressly bound for the same at a fixed period."

In connection with the establishment of the army bill office, a notification was made to the public by His Excellency, that James Green, Esquire, had been appointed Director, and Louis Montizambert, Esquire, Cashier, and that they had given the required security for the faithful performance of the trust reposed in them. The office was opened at the Court House, and from thence by order of His Excellency, an issue of army bills was made, consisting of the denominations, twenty-five dollars, fifty dollars, one hundred dollars and four hundred dollars; signed by His Excellency the Commander of the Forces, by the Director, by the Military Secretary and made payable to the bearer, on demand, at the army bill office, in Government bills of exchange at the current rate of exchange or in cash, at the option of the Commander of the Forces, with interest.

Prior to the passing of the "Act to facilitate the circulation of army bills," the currency of Canada consisted of a variety of coins. In the absence of a colonial coinage, the gold and silver coins of several nations were in circulation. Spanish, Portuguese, French and German, circulated simultaneously with the gold and silver coins of Great Britain. During the session of 1795, the following statute was passed, viz: "An Act to prevent the diminution of specie circulating in this Province, that the same may be regulated according to a standard that shall not present an advantage by carrying it to neighbouring countries; and whereas, by an ordinance now in force for regulating the currency of this Province, an advantage does arise by carrying gold coin out of the same, be it therefore enacted that the gold and silver coins hereafter mentioned, shall pass current and be deemed a legal tender in payment of al debts, and demands whatsoever in this Province, at the weights and rates following, that is to say :

NAMES OF COINS.	Weighing.		Canada Currency.		
	Dwts.	Grains.	£	s.	d.
The British guinea	5	6	1	3	4
The Johannes of Portugal.	18		4	0	0
The Moidore of Portugal......................	6	18	1	10	0
The Four Pistole piece of Spain.................	17		3	14	0
The French Louis d'or coined before 1793.	5	4	0	18	0
The American Eagle............................	11	6	2	10	0

With regard to silver, the American dollar shall pass current at five shillings currency, and every other coin current in the Province as already provided for, viz :

	Canada Currency.		
The Spanish dollar at.................................	£0	5	0
The British Crown..	0	5	6
The French Crown or piece of 6 livres Tournois....	0	5	6
The French piece of 4 livres, 10 sols......	0	4	2

	Canada Currency.		
The British shilling.	£0	1	1
The French piece of 24 sols Tournois.	0	1	1
Pistareen.....	0	1	0
The French piece of 36 sols Tournois....................	0	1	8

A similar Act was passed by the Parliament of Upper Canada on the 3rd of June, 1796.

Great inconvenience was experienced in consequence of the scarcity of specie, which gave rise to a kind of barter, or store pay, prejudicial to the interests of the farmers and labouring classes. Farm produce, furs, and labour were paid for in goods which had to be taken at unreasonably high prices at the shops or stores, because specie was hardly to be had.

Under the Army Bill Act, however, a paper currency was introduced, which proved of essential service, not only in meeting the exigencies of the public service, but in facilitating commercial transactions. The measure proved, in practice, a complete success. Bills of the denominations $25, $50, $100 and $400 were not re-issued. They bore interest, as provided for in the Act, $400, fourpence per diem, $100, one penny per diem, $50, one halfpenny per diem, and $25, one farthing per diem, being substantially interest at the rate of [six per cent. per annum.]

Four dollar bills bore no interest, and they were re-issued. They were payable at the army bill office in cash on demand.

Many years ago I ascertained from merchants who were engaged in the retail business in Quebec in 1812, and during the war, that the army bills circulated freely, the larger denominations with interest from the date of issue added. The calculation of interest which had accrued was an easy one : $400 for 30 days was just 120 pence, equal to 10 shillings currency ; $100, 30 pence ; $50, 15 pence, and so on ; consequently the increased value of each bill was easily ascertained ; and it passed, with its increment, from one to another in the purchase of goods or settlement of account.

The Act provided for the redemption of bills of $25 and upwards, in cash or exchange on London, at 30 days sight, at the option of the Commander of the forces, at the current rate of exchange ; but the interest which had accrued on all such bills was paid in cash or exchange at the option of the holder.

The current rate of exchange for bills on London at 30 days sight was established once in every fortnight, by a committee of five persons named by His Excellency.

The rate of exchange for bills on London, in consequence of the suspension of specie payments by the Bank of England, which took place in 1797, and which lasted till 1823, was very low. This subject, however, has to be considered in connection with the price of gold in England.

The mint price of an ounce of Standard gold is £3 17s. 10½d., being one-twelfth part of £46 14s. 6d. the value set upon a pound weight of gold.

During the Napoleonic wars, the price of gold in England per ounce rose, in 1800 to £4.5s. currency; in 1809 to £4.11s.; in 1810 to £4.19s.; and in 1812, when Napoleon was in the zenith of his power, to £5.10s. British currency. In order therefore to effect a settlement in Canada on a specie basis, bills drawn at 30 days sight on the Treasury in London, were subject to a large discount, frequently as much as 22%, as determined by the committee appointed by His Excellency to regulate the rate of exchange. Consequently, a bill at 30 days sight for £100, at that rate, yielded only £78 sterling, equal to $356.46 in specie. In 1812 £100 sterling in gold in England was worth £120 4s. 9d.; in 1813, £100 sterling in gold was worth £122.18s. currency of Great Britain.

It has to be borne in mind that the dollar in gold of 1812, was of greater value than the dollar in gold of the present day, on account of its greater weight and fineness. It required only $4.57 to constitute the par of the pound sterling in 1812 ; whereas it requires $4.86⅝ to constitute the par now, being 9½% over the ninth or old par of Queen Anne. In other words, the American eagle of 1792 contained 247½ grains of fine gold—the American eagle of 1837 contains only 232.2 grains of fine gold. There has been no change since that year in the quality or weight of the American eagle.

In the early part of August 1812, the war, both by land and sea, began to assume its proper character. The American General, Hull, with a strong force, crossed from Detroit to the Canadian shore on the 12th of July. Hull, however, had calculated upon a friendly reception in Canada, but found the people hostile ; and, being warned of the advance of General Brock with a force of over 300 regulars, 400 militia, and several hundred Indians, led by Tecumseh, made a hasty retreat, recrossed the river and occupied his old quarters in Detroit. General Brock, however, with characteristic daring, crossed in pursuit, attacked and captured the town with 33 pieces of cannon, and the military chest ; and took General Hull and 2,500 troops prisoners of war.

During the autumn, several raids were made along the frontier of the Upper St. Lawrence, and at other points ; but none of them of any importance, and none of them very creditable to either party. The Americans were repulsed at Presqu'île on September the 16th ; Gananoque was raided by Americans on the 21st ; the British were repulsed at Ogdensburg on October the 4th ; and several British craft were captured off Black Rock, Lake Erie, on October the 9th.

In the early part of October, however, viz., on the 12th, General Van Renselaer, in command of a con siderable force of American regulars and militia on the Niagara frontier, prepared to attack the British at Queenston, opposite Lewiston. He considered his forces ample to secure success. They numbered more than six thousand. The British force on the Western bank of the Niagara river, regular, militia, and Indians, numbered fifteen hundred. The Indian allies, under John Brant, numbered about two hundred and fifty strong. In addition, there was a detachment of the 41st regiment, 380 strong, under Captain Bullock, and the flank companies of the 49th regiment.

The Americans effected a landing, notwithstanding a desperate resistance made by the British, and occupied the heights after a hot engagement, in which the gallant Brock lost his life ; but they were finally defeated and driven over the precipitous banks of the Niagara river at the point of the bayonet. About 1,100 Americans, officers and privates, surrendered unconditionally as prisoners of war.

CHAPTER II.

The Provincial Parliament of Lower Canada was summoned for the despatch of business on the 29th December, 1812. In the Speech from the Throne, His Excellency Sir George Prevost said :—

".The complete discomfiture of the plans of the enemy for the conquest of Upper Canada, by the capture of Detroit, and by the surrender of the whole invading army with its general ; the brilliant achievement at Queenston, tho' clouded by death in the hour of victory, of the gallant and much lamented Major-General Brock, together with other recent advantages gained over the enemy, both in Lower and Upper Canada, are subjects of sincere congratulations, and demand our fervent acknowledgments to the Great Ruler of the Universe for these undeserved mercies.

" I take also pleasure in acquainting you that the measure of the issue of army bills, for the circulation of which you so promptly and liberally provided during the last session, has been attended with the happiest effects, both by powerfully aiding His Majesty's Government to meet the extraordinary demands of the present crisis, and by materially facilitating commercial transactions. The experience of four months having fully shown the utility of the measure, I recommend to your consideration the adoption of such further regulations and provisions respecting it, as, upon a review of the Act passed upon this head, and of the present circumstances of the country, may appear to be necessary."

It is manifest, I have said, that the Act to facilitate the circulation of army bills, proved a complete success; but a much larger amount of notes than that authorized by the Act had been issued during the recess; and the [exigencies of the public service rendered it necessary to resort to a further increase of issue.]

At the fourth session of the seventh Parliament holden in Quebec the 29th December, 1812, "An Act to extend the provisions of an Act passed in the fifty-second year of His Majesty's reign, intituled, "An Act to facilitate the circulation of army bills," and to make further regulations respecting the same," was passed, and received the royal assent on the 15th February, 1813. The Act reads as follows:

I. Whereas an Act was made and passed in the fifty-second year of His Majesty's reign, intituled "An Act to facilitate the circulation of army bills;" And whereas it appears by a message of the Governor-in-Chief to the House of Assembly of the 8th

January, 1813, that the exigencies of the public
service have rendered it indispensably necessary for
him as Commander-in-Chief to direct an issue of the
army bills to be made to a greater amount than two
hundred and fifty thousand pounds provided for by
the said Act, and that the further exigencies of the
public service may render a further issue indispensably
necessary ; and whereas it is expedient to subject
such army bills as have been so issued, as well as
such as may be hereafter issued, to the provisions,
regulations, and enactments of the afore-recited Act,
and to make further provisions and regulations
respecting the same ; Be it therefore enacted by the
king's most Excellent Majesty, by and with the
advice and consent of the Legislative Council and
Assembly of the Province of Lower Canada, consti-
tuted and assembled, by virtue of and under the
authority of an Act of the Parliament of Great Britain,
passed in the 31st year of His Majesty's reign,
intituled " An Act to repeal certain parts of an Act
passed in the 14th year of His Majesty's reign,
intituled, "An Act for making more effectual provision
for the government of the Province of Quebec ;
in North America ;" "and to make further provision
for the government of the said Province, and it is
hereby enacted by the authority of the same, that all
army bills which have been so issued after the time
at which the army bills then issued, amounted to the
sum of two hundred and fifty thousand pounds, and
each and every of them and all such army bills as

shall be issued during the next twelve months, from and after the passing of this Act, shall be deemed and taken to be within the purview of the Act made and passed in the 52nd year of His Majesty's reign, intituled, "An Act to facilitate the circulation of army bills;" and that all the provisions, regulations and enactments in the said last-mentioned Act contained, and each and every of them, shall be applied and put in force in respect to all and every such army bills so issued, or that may hereafter be issued, as fully and effectually to all intents and purposes as if the same were severally and separately repeated, and herein recited, and made part of this Act under the restrictions hereinafter mentioned.

II. Provides for the payment out of all and every and any the monies, customs, taxes and revenues of this province, and in preference to all other claims and demands whatsoever, all such interest at the rate of fourpence per one hundred pounds per diem, as shall arise and grow due upon all and every and any army bill or bills, which have been issued, or shall hereafter be issued.

III. Provided always that the sum so to be paid out of and from the customs &c. aforesaid, with interest as aforesaid, shall not on the whole and together exceed the sum of fifteen thousand pounds currency per annum.

IV. Provided also, and be it further enacted by the authority aforesaid, that the amount of army bills in circulation as well as those already issued or such as may be hereafter issued, shall not at any one period exceed the sum of five hundred thousand pounds currency.

V. And be it further enacted by the authority aforesaid, that interest upon such army bills as have been, or shall hereafter be issued, shall run from the day of the date of such bill or bills, until the same shall be paid, and that the holder or holders of every such bill or bills shall be entitled to demand and receive payment of all such interest at stated periods, once in every six months, at the army bill office in the city of Quebec, and further, that public notification shall be given in the Quebec Gazette immediately after the passing of this Act, by order of the Governor, Lieutenant-Governor, or the person administering the government for the time being, of the periods at which such payments shall be made.

VI. And whereas it is expedient in order that the public confidence in such army bills may remain undiminished, that the holders thereof may be assured of the punctual payment of all interest that may become due and payable on army bills ; and whereas the sum of fifteen thousand pounds per annum herein before provided, may not suffice for the full payment thereof on the whole amount of bills so issued or to be issued, Be it therefore enacted, by the authority aforesaid, that the provisions, regulations and enactments of the Act herein before cited, intituled, "An Act to facilitate the circulation of army bills," shall not extend or be construed to extend to a greater amount of army bills in circulation at any one time, during the next twelve months after the passing of this Act, than two hundred and fifty thousand pounds currency, unless public notification shall be given in the Quebec Gazette within one month after the passing of this Act, by the Commander of His Majesty's forces in this province for the time being, that all such interest as aforesaid shall be paid at the army bill office at the like stated periods.

VII. And be it further enacted, that the five Commissioners heretofore appointed for the purpose of certifying the current rate of exchange, at which bills of exchange on London were and are to be given in payment of army bills, and their successors, or any three of them, shall continue to meet and certify under Oath the rate of exchange in like manner, and that in due execution of their office, as aforesaid, they shall be guided by the fair current rate of bills of exchange at thirty days' sight, and by all such other information as they may be able to procure, so as to enable them to do substantial justice to the holders of such bills, and to the government.

VIII. And be it further enacted, that it shall be the duty of the officer or officers to whom it may appertain as having the direction of the army bill office, to lay before the Commissioners immediately after the passing of this Act, a correct account of the amount of all such army bills as shall then be in circulation, and at each second subsequent meeting of the said Commissioners, a true and correct account of all such bills as shall have been issued and put into circulation from the date of the last account rendered, in order that the same may be laid before the Legislature, at its next ensuing meeting.

IX. And be it further enacted, that all sheriffs and bailiffs who shall or may receive army bills upon execution, shall be accountable for the interest on all such bills which by them or any of them shall be so received for, and during the time that such bills remain in their hands, to the persons interested therein, and to this end the said sheriffs and bailiffs shall mention in their respective returns, whether they received the amount or any part of the amount of such executions in money or in such bills, and also the day on which they received it.

X. And be it further enacted, that no public officer whatsoever shall profit by the interest on the army bills which may be placed in his hands as such public officer, to be given in payment, and shall render an account of the said interest, annually, on the first day of November, to the Receiver-General to be employed according to the dispositions of the fourth section of the aforesaid Act, passed in the fifty-second year of His Majesty's reign.

XI. And be it further enacted, that the interest for which the Receiver-General and collector and all public officers are accountable to the province, shall be employed and applied in the payment of the interest wherewith the Province is by this Act charged.

XII. Provided always, and be it further enacted, that nothing in this Act contained shall extend or be construed to extend or entitle any holder or holders of any such army bills as aforesaid, as may at any time hereafter, remain unpaid or unsatisfied (save and except the holder or holders of such army bills as were heretofore issued, subsequent to the passing of the Act, to facilitate the circulation of army bills and until the same exceeded in the whole the sum of two hundred and fifty thousand pounds, and which now remain unpaid and unsatisfied) to receive out of or from any monies that may then be in the hands of the Receiver-General of this Province, or from any monies that may hereafter come into his hands arising out of any taxes or duties heretofore imposed or that may hereafter be imposed, levied, or raised by virtue of any Act of the Provincial Legislature, or from the rents and revenues of His Majesty's territorial domains in this province, or from any other monies in the hands of the Receiver-General, payment of any such army bill or bills, as aforesaid.

XIII. And be it further enacted, that should the Governor-in-Chief deem it expedient, to cause the whole or any part of the army bills to be hereafter issued to be signed by any other person or persons, by and under his authority ; public notice shall be given during one month in the Quebec Gazette, of the name or names of such person or persons so authorised, and that all army bills signed by such person or persons, shall be considered as forming part of the sum of five hundred thousand pounds, at which the whole amount of army bills to be circulated at the same period is hereinbefore limited.

XIV. And be it further enacted, that the sum of five hundred thousand pounds, at which the amount of army bills to be in circulation at one period is limited, such amount may be issued in army bills of one, two, eight, ten, twelve, sixteen and twenty dollars each, as the Commander of the forces may deem expedient and necessary, such bills bearing no interest and payable in cash on demand at the army bill office. Provided always that the amount of such bills, and of bills of four dollars each, shall not in the whole and together exceed the sum of fifty thousand pounds.

XV. And be it further enacted, that it shall and and may be lawful for the Governor, as Commander of the forces, to establish such other office or offices at Montreal or elsewhere in the Province as to him may seem expedient and necessary for the payment of all such bills as have, or may hereafter be issued, payable in cash on demand. Provided that the whole expense thereby incurred, together with the expense of the office already established, do not in the whole exceed the sum of two thousand five hundred pounds per annum, appropriated by the Act herein before mentioned.

The following is a copy of advertisement respecting the adjustment of the rate of exchange :

C

"Quebec, 15th March, 1813.

"The Commissioners appointed by His Excellency Sir George Prevost, Governor-in-chief and Commander of the Forces, in virtue of the Provincial Act of the 52nd year of His Majesty's reign, intituled, "An Act to facilitate the circulation of army bills,' (the provisions thereof being extended, and further regulated by an Act of the 53rd year of His Majesty's reign) have fixed on the rate of exchange for government bills, at 30 days sight, at twenty per cent for the next fortnight from this date."

N.B.—"The said Commissioners meet every Monday fortnight at 10 o'clock, at the house of Mr. Blackwood, St. Louis Street, where written communications on the subject of exchange will be received and duly attended to."

The army bills of the denominations $400, $100, $50 and $25, were signed, as I have already stated, by His Excellency as Commander of the forces, by the Director, and by the Military Secretary, and made payable as provided for in the Act. The four dollar bills were signed by the director of the Army bill office, the Cashier and the military secretary only.

The whole of the bills were deposited in the military chest, from whence they were issued in payment of whatever demands were required to be made on the Commissary-General or Paymaster-General, on account of the public service.

The signing of these bills by His Excellency was apparently found inconvenient, for, under date of 23rd March, 1813, I find the following notice :

"His Excellency has directed that public notice be given, and the same is hereby given, that all such army bills, will, from and after the 24th day of April, instead of bearing the signature of His Excellency the Commander of the forces, be signed under the authority of His Excellency, by James Green, Esquire, director of the said army bill office, or by the director of the said office for the time being, by the command of His Excellency, and by Louis Montizambert, Esquire, cashier of the said office for the time being, and by those persons only."

And on the 22nd of April, further notice is given as follows :

"And whereas certain army bills now bearing my signature still remain to be issued, and will be issued, nothwithstanding the said notification, after the said 24th instant. I have therefore thought fit, by this proclamation, to make known the same, and the same is hereby made known accordingly." Given &c.,

Signed. George Prevost.

In 1813 the passenger traffic or intercourse between Quebec and Montreal was carried on by a line of stages, which set out every morning at four o'clock during the summer season, Mondays excepted ; but in the early part of May a steamer, named the "Swiftsure," was put on the river line. She started from Montreal at five o'clock on Saturday morning, anchored at eight o'clock the same evening near Three Rivers, which she left on Sunday morning at five o'clock, and arrived at the King's Wharf, Quebec, at half-past two ; being only about twenty-four hours and a half under way between the two cities, with a strong head wind all the way. The advertisement sets forth that she is superbly fitted up : "twenty-two berths in the great cabin, each sufficient for two passengers, besides four for ladies in the state room, and a separate room for families. In the steerage, a great number of passengers can be accommodated. America cannot boast a more useful and expensive undertaking by one individual than this of Mr. Molson."

"His Excellency the Governor-in-Chief set out for Montreal on Tuesday afternoon in the Steam Boat." On March the 20th, 1813, it was announced by the Foreign Office in London that the necessary measures had been taken for the blockade of the ports and harbours of New York, Charleston, Port Royal, Savannah, and of the river Mississippi. There was no lack of energy on either side in the prosecution of the war. Great activity prevailed in the port of Quebec. Between the 5th and 16th of June, sixty-one vessels in all arrived ; twenty-six in ballast, sixteen with general cargoes, five with government stores, and thirteen with passengers and troops ; the troops consisted of the Wattville regiment, the 89th, the 104th ; and one vessel had soldiers belonging to different regiments and some artillery on board. Halifax was also a busy port during the war ; there, ships of war held themselves ready for any emergency ; thither ships of war and privateers took the prizes taken at sea. In the cargo of one prize, the "Marquis de Somerlos," a case containing twenty-one paintings and fifty engravings, shipped by a Mr. J. A. Smith, was found, addressed, "*To the Academy of Arts, Philadelphia,*" a gift to that institution. The authorities at Halifax released the works of art and forwarded them to Philadelphia, "with the sincerest wishes for the success of the infant society," —in striking contrast to the conduct of Napoleon, who plundered the National Galleries of Europe, not even sparing the Vatican, and sent the paintings and statuary to Paris. But time at last makes all things even. "The Transfiguration and the Last Communion of St. Jerome resumed their place in the Vatican; the Apollo and the Laocoon again adorned the precincts of St. Peter's; the Venus was enshrined anew amid beauty in the tribune of Florence; and the Descent from the Cross, by Rubens, was restored to the devout worship of the Flemings in the Cathedral at Antwerp."

The Americans were nothing daunted by the reverse at Queenston. The authorities, as well as the writers, spoke of the death of Brock as equivalent to a victory. At the end of April, 1813, a joint land and naval expedition was organized to capture York (now Toronto) the capital of Upper Canada. The American fleet appeared before the town on the 26th, conveying a land force of 2,500 men. Toronto had for defence, under Major-General Sheaffe, less than 600 men, consisting of regulars and militia. General Pike, of the American army, at the head of a division of at least 1,000 strong, landed, in spite of a spirited resistance. The Americans swarmed into the old French fort and harbour defences, fiery with fighting, and flushed with success, when suddenly,—with the crash and concussion of an earthquake,—the powder magazine exploded at their feet, spreading havoc through their ranks. Of the assailants, 250 were instantly killed or wounded,—General Pike amongst the killed; of the defenders many perished. The contest itself was stayed by the catastrophe; it had endured eight

hours. The surviving British troops had withdrawn ;
all that could be done had been done, and York
capitulated through the local officers of militia.
Sheaffe left behind him, of regulars sixty-two killed
and seventy-two wounded. The Americans kept
possession, but evacuated York on the 2nd of May,
1813.*

The complete victory of the Americans over the
British at York atoned in some measure for the
reverse they had suffered at Queenston Heights. I
might now allude to the success of the Americans at
sea, to their victory over the British frigate Guerrière;
to the naval duel between the British ship Shannon
and the American Chesapeake, to the defeat and
capture of the latter after a sanguinary engagement ;
but it is not my intention to refer to the stirring
events of the war, further than may seem to me desirable to show the necessity which existed for the
Army Bill Act, and for the subsequent enlargement
of its provisions to meet the exigencies of the public
service.

Several raids or attacks were made from both sides
of the lines with alternate successes and defeats.
Among the most memorable were the attack on
Sackets harbour by the British, without any satisfactory result ; the capture of Fort George by the
Americans ; the subsequent night attack by the British
upon the American army encamped at Stoney-creek,

---

* Colonel Coffin, " 1812, Chronicle of the War."

where deadly work was done with the bayonet, in the lurid light of the watch-fires, as the sleepers aroused, rose stumbling and dazed. Two American Generals, caught napping, and one hundred soldiers were made prisoners of war. The rest of the American Army made a hasty retreat, never halting till safe within the works of Fort George. But the most memorable of all the engagements was the battle of Chateauguay in October 1813, when a powerful invading force of Americans, bent upon the subjugation of Lower Canada, was beaten back and signally defeated by a small force, consisting chiefly of French Canadian militia, led by Colonel de Sala- berry. There was also a minor engagement at Cryslers farm, in which the Americans were defeated.

The expenses connected with the war were so great that it is difficult to conceive how it could have been carried on without the operation of the Army Bill Act. We are, I believe, as much indebted to the authors of that measure for the preservation of our connection with the British Empire, as we are to the valour of our soldiers and sailors in repelling a cruel and unwarrantable invasion.

The Provincial Parliament again assembled on the 13th of January, 1814. His Excellency Sir George Prevost, after alluding in his Speech from the throne to His Majesty's victorious arms in Europe, said: "In turning our eyes to our own shores, we have abundant cause for gratitude to the Supreme Giver of all good, for the termination of the late campaign in a manner so glorious to the British arms, and so disastrous to those of the enemy.

"The defeat sustained by him on the Chateauguay, where a handful of brave Canadians repelled a powerful division of his army ; and the brilliant victory obtained by a small corps of observation on the banks of the St. Lawrence, (Crysler's farm) have at the same time upheld the honour of His Majesty's arms, and effectually disconcerted all the plans of the enemy for the invasion of the Province."

On the 25th of January, 1814, the thanks of the House of Assembly were voted to Lieutenant-Colonel de Salaberry, and to the officers and privates under his command in the engagement at Chateauguay on the 26th October, 1813 ; and to Lieutenant-Colonel Morrison of the 89th regiment, and the officers and privates under his command at Crysler's farm on the 11th November.

On the 5th of February, the speaker informed the House that he had received from Lieutenant-Colonel de Salaberry a letter, in return to the thanks of the House to him, which he read.

The letter is a remarkably able composition, of which I cannot refrain from inserting one paragraph :

"In preventing the enemy from penetrating into the province, one common sentiment animated the whole of my three hundred brave companions, and in which I participated, that of doing our duty, serving our Sovereign, and saving our country from the evil of an invasion. The satisfaction arising from our success was to us adequate recompense ; but we now enjoy another of inestimable value, in the distinguished honour conferred in the thanks voted to us by the House of

Assembly. This generous proceeding leaves in our minds an impression, deep, lively, and indelible. The country, through its representatives, evincing itself thus nobly grateful, requites the service of its children with the highest and most flattering reward."

On the 17th of January, 1814, His Excellency sent a message to the House, stating that the exigencies of the public service rendered it necessary that he should direct a further and more extensive issue of army bills. Accordingly an Act, further to extend the provisions of the two Acts for facilitating the circulation of army bills, was introduced.

The preamble runs as follows :—

"Whereas an Act was made and passed in the fifty-second year of His Majesty's reign, intituled, "'An Act to facilitate the circulation of army bills,'" and whereas, another Act was made and passed in the fifty-third year of His Majesty's reign, intituled, "'An Act to extend the provisions of an Act made and passed in the fifty-second year of His Majesty's reign, intituled, "An Act to facilitate the circulation of army · bills," and to make further regulations respecting the same,'" and that by the fourth clause of the last mentioned Act, it is provided and enacted, that no greater sum than five hundred thousand pounds currency in army bills, shall be in circulation at any one time. And whereas it appears by His Excellency the Governor-in-Chief's message to the House of Assembly of the 17th January, that the exigencies of the public service render it indispensably necessary that he, as Commander of the forces, should direct a further and more extensive issue of army bills to be made. And whereas it also appears by the accounts of the Director of the army bill office laid before the House of Assembly, that a greater sum in army bills has been and now remains in circulation than the aforesaid sum of five hundred thousand pounds, and that it is expedient and necessary to extend the provisions of the said Acts to all such army bills as now are in circulation, and to a further issue to be made, to make further regulations respecting the same, and also to indemnify all persons concerned in the making and issuing of army bills, over and above the said sum of five hundred thousand pounds ; be it therefore enacted, by the King's Most Excellent Majesty, by and with the advice and consent of the Legislative Council and Assembly of the Province of Lower Canada. It is hereby enacted that from and after the passing of this Act, all army bills issued heretofore and now in circulation, or which shall be made and issued at the army bill office in the City of Quebec, from and after the passing of this Act, until the first day of February, 1815, shall be deemed and taken to be within the purview of the Act made and passed in the fifty-second year of His Majesty's reign, intituled, "An Act to facilitate the circulation of army bills," subject, nevertheless, to the restrictions contained in the Act made and passed in the fifty-third year of His Majesty's reign, intituled, "An Act to extend the provisions of an Act made and passed in the fifty-second year of His Majesty's reign, intituled, "An Act to facilitate the circulation of army bills," and to make further regulations respecting the same," and that all provisions, regulations and enactments in the said Acts contained, (save and except as aforesaid) and each and every of them shall be applied and put in force in respect to all and every such army bills so issued, or that may hereafter be issued, as fully and effectually to all intents and purposes as if the same were severally and separately repeated, and herein recited and made part of this Act, in so far as the said provisions and enactments are not hereinafter altered or repealed.

II. Provided always, and be it further enacted by the authority aforesaid, that the amount of army bills in circulation, as well those already made and issued as such as may hereafter be made and issued, shall not at any one period exceed the sum of fifteen hundred thousand pounds, current money of this province.

III. And whereas it is essential for the security of the persons who may become possessed of army bills to be issued as aforesaid, and in order to assure to such persons the advantages conferred on the said bills by this Act, and to promote the public confidence in the said bills, that the aforesaid limitation prescribed to the issue of the said bills shall be strictly adhered to, and under no circumstances infringed ; Be it therefore enacted, by the authority aforesaid, that the Director of the army bill office, the Cashier of the said office, and any other officer or officers concerned in the making, signing and issuing of the army bills to be issued as aforesaid, for the time being, shall in no instance and under no circumstances whatever, make, sign or issue any such army bill or army bills, when and so long as the army bills in circulation shall amount in value to, and not be less than fifteen hundred thousand pounds, current money of the Province.; and that if the said Director of the army bill office, the Cashier of the said office or any other officer or officers concerned in the making, signing or issuing of army bills so to be issued as aforesaid for the time being, shall make, sign, or issue any army bill or army bills after the said army bills already issued and to be issued and in circulation at the same time, shall amount to fifteen hundred thousand pounds, such Director of the army bill office, Cashier of the said office, and other officer or officers concerned in the making, signing, or issuing of army bills beyond that amount, shall thereby be rendered incapable of serving His Majesty, in any office, civil or military in this Province ; and shall moreover severally and respectively forfeit to His Majesty, his heirs and successors, the amount of all such army bills as shall have been made, signed and issued over and beyond the said limitation of fifteen hundred thousand pounds, to be recovered by action of debt, bill, plaint or information in any of His Majesty's courts of Record in this Province ; one moiety whereof, when recovered, shall be to and for the use of our Sovereign Lord the King, his heirs and successors, and the other moiety thereof (with all costs of suits) to and for the use of such person or persons as shall inform or sue for the same ; and that in default of goods, chattels, land and tenements out of and from which the money so forfeited may be levied, such Director of the army bill office, Cashier, officer or officers as aforesaid, against whom judgment may be rendered for the money so forfeited, shall be taken and conveyed into the common gaol of the district in which such judgment shall be rendered, and there detained, until he or they, respectively, do pay the amount of such judgment, any law, usage, or custom to the contrary notwithstanding.

IV. And be it further enacted by the authority aforesaid, that each and every of such army bills, as aforesaid, shall and may be received and taken, and shall pass and be current to all and every the collectors and receivers in this Province of Lower Canada, of the customs or any revenue or tax whatsoever already due or payable, or which shall or may hereafter be granted, due or payable to His Majesty, his heirs and successors, under and by virtue of any Act of the Parliament of Great Britain, or of the Provincial Parliament or otherwise ; and also at the office of the Receiver-General of this Province, from the said collectors and receivers, or from any other person or persons, bodies politic or corporate whatsoever making any payments whatsoever to His Majesty, his heirs and successors, for, upon any account, causes or occasion whatsoever, and that the same in the hands of such collectors and receivers, and in the hands of the Receiver-General of this Province, shall be deemed and taken as if paid in the gold or silver coin passing current in this Province, and as such, shall be charged against and credited to such collector and receiver, and to such Receiver-General as aforesaid, respectively, in their respective accounts with each other, and with His Majesty, his heirs and successors.

V. And be it further enacted by the authority aforesaid, that the interest which from time to time shall be due upon any such army bill, as aforesaid, shall be allowed to all persons, bodies politic and corporate, paying the same to the Receiver-General of this Province, or to any collector or receiver of any of His Majesty's customs, revenues or taxes up to the respective days whereupon such bill or bills shall be so paid; provided always, that every such Receiver-General, collectors and receivers as aforesaid, shall be accountable for the interest on every such bill by them or either of them received, for and during the time during which such bill shall remain in their hands.

VI. Imposes penalty on forging bills, and provides that such person or persons so forging and offending, being thereof lawfully convicted, shall be adjudged a felon, and shall suffer as in cases of felony, without benefit of clergy.

VII. Sets forth the penalty in persons stealing army bills.

VIII. Enacts that contracts shall be void in which

any distinction shall be made between army bills
and cash.

IX. Provides that no arrest shall be made if a
tender in army bills be made.

X. No attachment shall issue if there be not an
affidavit of no tender in army bills.

XI. On *capias ad satisfaciendum,* a deposit of the
debt and costs in army bills shall stay proceedings.

XII. On *fieri facias,* etc., a deposit of the debt and
costs in army bills shall stay proceedings.

XIII. And be it further enacted by the authority
aforesaid, that of the amount of army bills now in
circulation, and hereafter to be issued a sum no less
than two hundred thousand pounds, and not exceeding five hundred thousand pounds, shall be in bills of
one, two, three, five and ten dollars, such bills payable
as those of larger denominations, in bills of exchange
on London, and not bearing interest, and that the
holders of such bills shall be entitled to demand, and
receive at the army bill office on demand, army bills
of fifty dollars and upwards, bearing interest for the
amount of all such bills.

XIV. And be it further enacted by the authority
aforesaid, that during three months, to be computed
from the passing of this Act, it shall and may be
lawful to and for all and every person in possession
of army bills of the value of twenty-five dollars only,
bearing interest to have and receive at the army bill
office on demand, bills of one, two, three, five and ten
dollars, in exchange for such army bills of twenty-

five dollars, together with the interest due and payable
thereon, up to the day of making such exchange.
Provided always that the Director of the army bill
office, or those employed under him, in exchanging the
said army bill, shall not, during the said three months
next after the passing of this Act, be bound so to
exchange such army bills to a greater amount in any
one day than that of two hundred and fifty pounds ;
provided also, that the same person shall not, in any
one week, require to be so exchanged, more than one
army bill of twenty-five dollars, bearing interest as
aforesaid.

XV. And be it further enacted, that it shall be
the duty of the officer or officers to whom it may
appertain, as having the direction of the army bill
office, to lay before the commissioners immediately
after the passing of this Act, a correct account of the
amount of all such army bills as shall then be in
circulation, and at each second subsequent meeting
of the said commissioners, a true and correct account
of all such bills as shall have been issued and put in
circulation from the date of the last account rendered,
in order that the same may be laid before the legislature at its next ensuing meeting.

XVI. Provided always, that nothing in this Act
contained, shall extend or be construed to extend
to entitle any holder or holders of any such army
bills as aforesaid, as may, at any time hereafter remain
unpaid or unsatisfied save and except the holder or
holders of such army bills as were heretofore issued,

subsequent to the passing of the " Act to facilitate the circulation of army bills," and until the same exceeded, on the whole, the sum of two hundred and fifty thousand pounds, and which now remain unpaid and unsatisfied, to receive out of or from any monies that there may be in the hands of the Receiver-General in this province, or from any monies that may hereafter come into his hands, arising out of any taxes or duties heretofore imposed, or that may hereafter be imposed, levied or raised by virtue of any Act of the Provincial Legislature, or from the rents and revenues of His Majesty's territorial domains in this province, or from any other monies in the hands of the Receiver-General, payment of any such army bill or bills as aforesaid.

XVII. And be it further enacted, that the director of the army bill office, and all and every person or persons aiding or assisting him in the issuing of army bills over and above the sum of five hundred thousand pounds, as limited by the Act fifty-third, George III., Ch. III., shall be freed, discharged and indemnified as well against the King's Majesty, his heirs and successors, as against all and every other person or persons, of, for, or concerning the making and issuing of all, any and every such army bills, as shall have been so made and issued beyond the said limitation.

The pacification of Europe did not now appear to be a remote issue. The disastrous defeat of the French army at Leipsic, and subsequent reverses, had weakened the resources of Napoleon. The

D

alliance between Austria, Russia and Prussia, proved a too formidable combination for him to cope with. Wellington was driving Soult from Spain, and British troops entered France on the 7th October, 1813. Paris surrendered to the allies on the 31st of March, 1814. The abdication of Napoleon was negotiated at Fontainebleau on the 5th of April, 1814. Louis the XVIII. arrived in Paris on the 3rd of May, and on the 4th, Napoleon embarked on board the British frigate Undaunted, an exile for Elba.

Great Britain, in prolonged conflict with France and her allies, under so great a leader of armies as Napoleon, had become burthened with a heavy debt. The bank of England had suspended specie payments. Gold in relation to the currency of the realm was at a high premium.

In October, 1813, the ounce of standard gold stood at £ 5 9s. currency.
In March, 1814,   "   "   "   5 8s.   "
In April,   "   "   "   "   5 5s.   "
In June,   "   ".   "   "   4 10s.   "
and the average price for the months of September, October, November and December, was £4.7s. currency.

From February, 1814 to July 1814, the rate of Exchange on London in Quebec for 30 days sight bills, was announced by the commissioners from time to time at 19% discount, but the prospect of peace sent the rate down. The rate of exchange in those days was not governed by the balance of trade, but by the issue of battles.

In August	1st,	1814, the discount was	16%.
"	15th,	" "	14%
"	29th,	" "	12%
Septr.	12th,	" "	10%
Octr.	11th,	" "	8%
"	24th,	" "	5%
Decr.	6th,	" "	2½%

The escape of Napoleon from Elba, on the first of March, 1815, and the consequent apprehension of a renewal of hostilities, sent the price of gold in England again up to £5.7s. ; and in sympathy with the fall in the value of current money in England, the discount on bills of exchange in Canada rose in July to 15%, but rallied towards the end of the month, when the rate was quoted at 10% discount.

On the 21st of January, 1815, at one o'clock, His Excellency the Governor-in-Chief came down in state to the Legislative Council to open the first session of the eighth Parliament. The Gentleman Usher of the Black Rod was sent down to the Assembly to command the attendance of that House, and the members being present, the Honourable Speaker of the Legislative Council signified His Excellency's pleasure that they should return and choose a fit person to be their Speaker, and present him to His Excellency on Tuesday the 24th, at one o'clock.

On that day, His Excellency being seated on the throne, and the Assembly, with Mr. Papineau, their speaker elect, being in attendance below the Bar, the Honourable the Speaker of the Legislative Council expressed His Excellency's allowance of the choice of the House of Assembly.

In the Speech from the throne, His Excellency alludes to the reinforcements he had received from His Majesty's Government, which enabled him to diminish the pressure of war on the inhabitants of the Province—and also to the demands of "the public service continuing various and large," and that he looks to Parliament for continued exertions to meet them,—for a renewal of a productive revenue bill, and of such of the provisions of the army bill act, as it shall be deemed expedient to adopt for the future.

With reference to the "Act to facilitate the circulation of army bills" and the two subsequent Acts extending the provisions thereof, I may remind my readers that the original act provided that a sum of fifteen thousand pounds should be forthcoming from the Provincial Exchequer, for the payment of interest on the first issue of army bills, amounting to two hundred and fifty thousand pounds, and also provincial security for the ultimate payment of army bills to that amount, if such army bills should remain unpaid at the expiration of five years.

The first Act to extend the provisions of the original Act, which authorizes an increased issue of army bills to the amount of two hundred and fifty thousand pounds currency—the whole issue not to exceed five hundred thousand pounds, limits the whole provision for interest to be paid out of the Provincial Exchequer to fifteen thousand pounds currency per annum, and gives no security or pledge for the ultimate payment of army bills beyond that for the first issue of two hundred and fifty thousand pounds.

The second Act to extend the provisions of the original Act, authorizes an issue, in all, of fifteen hundred thousand pounds ; but gives no security for the payment of interest on any amount of army bills in excess of two hundred and fifty thousand pounds as set forth and authorized in the original Act of 1st of August, 1812.

CHAPTER III.

The Americans contemplated, with no little apprehension, the pacification of Europe which followed the defeat of Napoleon at Leipsic and his subsequent exile to Elba. They once thought that there would be no difficulty in annexing Canada, that the war, for them, would be a mere promenade ; but instead of annexing Canada, Canada annexed the whole territory of Michigan, and administered its civil Government. And now that peace in Europe had apparently been restored and had set free the veterans of the British army for other service, the Americans considered that they had just cause for apprehension. The President at once communicated with several Governors of States. In July, 1814, he wrote : " Great Britain will now have a large disposable force, both naval and military, and with it, the means of giving the war in America a character of new and increased activity and extent ; " and as a measure of precaution he deems it advisable to strengthen themselves, and the line of the Atlantic, and invites the executive of certain states to organize, and hold in readiness for immediate service, a corps of ninety thousand five hundred men.

In anticipation of a prolonged state of warfare, for which the Americans were preparing, the committee upon the army bills, report to the House of Assembly on Friday the 17th of February, 1815, that it is ex-pedient to renew the provisions of the two Acts with some modifications, and to increase the amount of army bills which may be in circulation to £2,000,000 currency ; and the house having concurred, a bill was read the first time—second reading fixed for Monday the 20th. On that day the bill was read again, and referred to a general committee for discussion on Wednesday the 22nd, when some progress was made : the bill to be further discussed on Friday the 24th. On Monday the 27th, the committee report the amendments, and the house having concurred, it is ordered that the bill, thus amended, be engrossed. On Tuesday the 28th, the bill, as amended, for facili-tating the circulation of army bills, was read a third time, and passed the House of Assembly. But the bill was thrown out in the Upper House for reasons which shall presently appear.

On the 1st March, 1815, however, a message was received from His Excellency the Governor-in-Chief, acquainting the House of the Ratification of the Treaty of Peace. This was the Peace of Ghent, concluded between Great Britain and the United States, made substantially on the *status quo ante bellum*, and signed on the 24th December, 1814.

In the Canadian Archives there is the following report respecting the working of the Army Bill Act, showing the amount of bills in circulation in February, 1815.

Copy of report *re* amount of army bills in circulation in Febuary, 1815, together with the report of the board upon the subject.

"Quebec, 19th February, 1815.

"We, the undersigned, having assembled at Your Excellency's desire for the purpose of considering the subject of army bills in circulation, and having had reference to the several representations your Excellency has made to His Majesty's Government thereon, we have great satisfaction in stating that all the beneficial effects of the measure which have from time to time been anticipated by Your Excellency, have been fully realized ; in illustration of which the following calculations are submitted. At present there are about £800,000 in circulation in bills bearing interest, being a total of £1,300,000 ; the interest annually upon the £800,000 at 6 per cent is £48,000, deduct paid by the province £15,000, leaving a balance of £33,000, which is the total interest paid from the army extraordinaries for the use of £1,300,000, being a trifle more than 2½ per cent per annum—into this, calculation may also be taken to show the advantage derived by the public, that the loss upon exchange which has fluctuated from 2½ to 22½ per cent. discount, has been altogether saved upon the sum now in circulation, and what further loss the public must have sustained by the exchange, but for the relief afforded by this paper medium, it is not possible to calculate, no doubt it would have been enormous ; another advantage not to be overlooked, is the facility with which army bills have been conveyed to the most remote parts of this extensive command, to meet the exigencies of the service at an inconsiderable expense and risk, whereas the transport of specie would have been attended with danger, delay and heavy cost, besides which, the enemy has been deprived of his booty in two instances in his predatory incursions into Upper Canada, by the facility with which the contents of the military chests at York and Fort George were destroyed, without any loss to the public. In explanation of this circumstance it is necessary to observe that as the army bills do not become cash by the system adopted, until they are issued and dated, and the numbers of the bills having been kept by the accountants, they were replaced from the army bill office, or a similar amount in lieu thereof.

Understanding that another bill is in progress in the Provincial Legislature now in session, extending the provisions of the former Army Bill Acts, by which a further sum of £500,000 in bills not bearing interest may be issued, which, ad le l to the £1,300,000 at present in circulation, will make a total of £1,800,000, reducing thereby the interest paid the government for the use of this gross sum to a little more than 1¾ per cent. per annum.

The total expense of the army bill office establishment for the last year, amounted to about £4,000, £2,500 of which is defrayed by the Province, and the remaining £1,500 from the military chest. In all probability, this excess of £1,500 will be more than covered by the accidental loss of army bills, which, from the large amount in circulation, cannot fail of being very considerable.

In August 1817, it is provided by the first Army Bill Act that the province will no longer pay interest upon army bills that the holders may demand specie for them, and that the Governor may at any time previous to that period, call in and redeem with specie the army bills in circulation ; it is for the consideration of Your Excellency, how far it may be expedient to suggest to His Majesty's government to avail itself of any favorable circumstance of furnishing specie for this purpose upon advantageous terms in the course of the ensuing two years, to provide for the redemption of these bills, without waiting the expiration of the period prescribed by the Act.

These suggestions and calculations are submitted for your Excellency's consideration, but the inferences we have drawn will be rendered more conclusive when the state of public affairs will be known with more certainty, when the Army Bill Act shall have passed, when Your Excellency shall have received on the 27th inst. the periodical report of the commissioners for fixing the rate of exchange, and the next monthly account of the amount of bills in circulation from the director of the army bill office.

(Signed) W. H. ROBINSON,
      Com^y Genl.
(Signed) J. HALE,
      Dep.-Paymaster Genl.
(Signed) NOAH FREER,
      Military Secretary.

The bill referred to in the foregoing report as in
progress in the Provincial Parliament was thrown out
in the Upper House ; and I find a letter in the Quebec
Gazette of the 31st March, 1815, respecting its rejection, headed :

ARMY BILLS.

The fate of the new Army Bills Act, lately passed by the House of
Assembly and rejected by the legislative council, having excited public
curiosity, we are happy in being enabled by a correspondent, to gratify
our readers with the following observations on that interesting subject.

The Act of 1814. authorised the issue of army bills up to the 1st day
of February, 1815, to an amount not exceeding £1,500,000 currency at
any one time in circulation. This Act remains in full force in respect
to all bills issued within the above limits, and will continue in force
until the end of five years, counting from August 1812, and by the
monthly returns from the army bill office laid before the legislature, it
appears, that the above sum of £1,500,000 was amply sufficient for
the public service in both provinces, the largest amount stated to be in
circulation at any period during the last year being only about
£1,205,000.

At the time this Act was passed, the public were suffering for want
of small money ; a clause was therefore inserted, requiring that, of the
amount so to be issued, a sum not less than £200,000 nor more than
£500,000, should be issued in small bills bearing no interest—and at the
same time, to guard against the pernicious effects of a superabundance
of small bills in circulation, a proviso was wisely added, entitling the
holders of such bills, "to demand and receive at the army bills office,
on demand, army bills of $50 and upwards, bearing interest for the
amount of all such bills." This proviso is still in force but was wholly
omitted in the new bill.

Immediately after the passing of this Act on the 17th of March,
1814, the issue of small bills commenced, and was continued through
the summer and fall, and by the end of November, it would appear the
circulation of both Provinces was more than fully supplied, for early in
the following month we find by the monthly returns, that the public
began for the first time to avail themselves of the above proviso, by
bringing in small bills in exchange for large ones. Accordingly it

appears, that between the 12th of December, 1814, and 31st of January, 1815, no less than £43,925 was issued in large notes bearing interest, in exchange for small ones. As there is no reason to suppose that government exceeded the limits prescribed by the Act, here is plain proof that even half a million in small notes was more than sufficient for the circulation of both Provinces, seeing that in about ten months no less than £44,000 worth of them were brought back in exchange for large bills, exclusive of what were paid in during that period for bills of exchange. The presumption therefore is, that a smaller sum would have been quite sufficient during the war, and that a still smaller sum might suffice during peace.

Here it may be proper to remark, that the operation of the above proviso had the most salutary effect, by counteracting any excessive issue of small bills, and to this circumstance, in conjunction with the management of the exchange commissioners, may fairly be attributed the high and unprecedented degree of credit in which the paper hath hitherto been so happily maintained.

With this experience before our eyes, the object of the framers and advocates of the new army bill is altogether inconceivable. It began by extending the authority to issue army bills to an amount not exceeding £2,000,000 at any one time in circulation. This extension was surely unnecessary in a time of peace ; seeing that the former limits afforded more than sufficient for the public service, even during war. But this was not the principal objection to the bill.

In a subsequent clause it was enacted, that of the amount so to be issued, a sum not less than one million should be issued in small notes, bearing no interest, and the wise proviso in the former Act, for converting small notes into large ones, was entirely omitted. This extraordinary clause having passed in the Assembly, and the bill arrived at the third reading, a rider was proposed and agreed to, in that House, authorising the Commander of the forces, at any time, to buy up with cash, the whole or any part of the army bills bearing interest, whenever he might think proper.

In this shape the bill made its appearance in the Legislative Council, where, luckily, the members were too well acquainted with the subject to suffer its dangerous imperfections to escape their notice.

The words " not less than one million " were the first that struck their attention. By that clause as it originally stood, government might have issued the whole two million in small notes, at same time that they were authorized by the rider to buy up all the large ones. But a communication having taken place between the two houses, it was agreed to consider the words " not less " as a clerical error, and to substitute in their stead the words " not exceeding " which was accordingly done in a private way by the two speakers, etc. This was considerable im- provement to the clause, but it was liable to insurmountable objections, for want of the old proviso so often mentioned, to relieve the circulation from superfluous small notes there being no other mode of redemption provided than that of bills of exchange on London, which are only wanted by a very small portion of the community, and therefore, the issue of small notes to the extent of one million, must inevitably have produced a depreciation, seeing by the experience of last year, while the war expenditure was going on to its full extent, that even half a million was too much. Had the Legislative Council been at liberty to amend this bill, by inserting the old proviso for converting the superfluous small bills into large ones, everything would have found its level by means of that salutary check, and all might have gone well—but unfor- tunately, this all along had been considered (very erroneously) as a money bill, which the Upper House must not touch, and therefore they had no other option than to pass it or reject it. We do not pretend to give any report of the debates in council on this subject, but we understand it was very fully discussed during several sittings, and that finally the members were unanimous in rejecting the bill, as being the safer of the two alternatives.

The introduction of this paper currency, at the commencement of the late war with the United States, as the substitute for specie, at a time when there was very little specie in the country, and when the public service could not have been carried on without it, was certainly a seasonable and judicious experiment, and its unprecedented success has not only been a great pecuniary saving to Great Britain, but it has also contributed in no small degree to the preservation of these Provinces.

The credit of this paper ought, therefore, to be considered as an object of the first importance and carefully supported to the last, being a most valuable resource, to be again resorted to by government on future occasions in case of need. Mistaken notions of economy in attempting to save the interest by buying up the large bills and making excessive issues of small ones, if carried into practice, would be fraught with most dangerous consequences, and ought always to be resisted, for when depreciation begins, there is no knowing to what extent it may go, and the credit of the paper once lost will be remembered for a century to come, and render it impossible again to resume the system with any success.

Finding by experience that this paper is so advantageous to Great Britain, while at the same time it affords accommodation to moneyed men in this colony, some well-informed persons are of opinion, that it would be good policy to continue the system in peace as well as in war, and have expressed their surprise that no steps were taken after the rejection of the New Army Bill Act, to introduce a short bill, to authorize a further issue of army bills for a limited time, under the Act of 1814, which it is supposed would have met with no opposition in either house, the provisions of that Act having been found by experience to answer every desirable purpose. And we confess we are much inclined to this opinion, when we reflect that Great Britain has no money lying idle—that on the contrary, she is paying many millions annually for the interest of what she owes as a nation, and that she cannot send specie or anything else to this country, without adding so much, in some shape or other, to her national debt. It is true, the legal interest in England is only $5^o/_o$, while here it is $6^o/_o$. But it must at same time be recollected, that all our paper serves as a substitute for specie, that only about two-thirds of what is at present in circulation bears interest, and that the Province contributes £15,000 per annum towards that interest. To this must be added the advance of money in England (equal to perhaps six or eight months interest) and the ordinary expenses of purchasing and sending out the specie—and it must also be recollected that specie as a circulating medium, frequently finds its way into the neighbouring States, and therefore requires a frequent supply to keep up the requisite quantity, while, on the contrary, our paper remains at home, and requires only a judicious regulation of the rate of exchange, and due precaution against forgery to keep it in full credit.

Further to illustrate these observations, we have only to present our readers with the following statement in round numbers, which, by the returns from the army bill office, cannot be very far from the truth.

Suppose £1,200,000 in army bills at present in circulation. Of which £800,000 bears interest at 6%, £48,000, and £400,000 bearing no interest, being small bills, £1,200,000. Deduct so much paid by the Province £15,000, balance of interest (being only 2¾% on £1,200,000),—£33,000. Suppose bullion at the mint prices, and that Great Britain were to purchase and send out specie for the redemption of all these army bills, the expenses in freight on £1,200,000 cannot be less than 1½%, say £18,000, one year's interest on £1,200,000 @ 5%, £60,000—£78,000.

Deduct the foregoing balance of interest..................£33,000

Loss to Great Britain by sending out specie exclusive of the
risk and advance of money...............................£45,000

Thus it appears that Great Britain gets a substitute for specie in Canada to the amount of £1,200,000, for which she pays 2¾% per annum, and that it would cost her at least £45,000 to replace that substitute with specie !

Where can Great Britain get so advantageous a loan?

But even supposing the whole of our army bills were to bear interest —still we are of opinion that they would be advantageous to Great Britain, particularly when it is considered, that without them, we should require an annual supply of specie to a certain extent, to keep up the requisite quantity for circulation.

Expense of sending out £1,200,000 in specie as above
stated, including one year's interest................... £78,000

£1,200,000 in army bills, all bearing 6% interest. £72,000

Deduct so much paid by the Province.......... 15,000   57,000

Balance saved to Great Britain, supposing that all our bills
bore interest.....................................   21,000

Again we may ask where can Great Britain obtain a cheaper loan ?

N.B. What is meant by the " advance of money " is the difference between the time when money would be paid in England for the purchase of specie to send here, and the time at which bills drawn here for the public service get home and become due, which, in the ordinary course, is found on an average to be six or eight months—and the interest for that time is of course so much more to be added in favour of our army bills, which are only issued when they are wanted, and Great Britain is so much more the gainer. It would be easy to prove that at least half a million has been saved to Great Britain in one way or other, by means of our army bills up to this date.—Quebec, 24th March, 1815.

The following statements relating to the circulation of the army bills, copied from official documents in the Canadian Archives Bureau, will prove interesting to professional bankers.

Circulation of Army Bills.   ARMY BILL OFFICE,

24th April, 1815.

ACCOUNT OF THE AMOUNT OF ARMY BILLS IN CIRCULATION.

Balance of army bills remaining in circulation the 27th
March, 1815...£1,249,996   5

DEDUCT :—

So much redeemed by bills of exchange on London
since the 27th March, 1815, viz. :—

In large bills.............. ...£   43 15
In small bills 3,594   5 £ 3,638   0
175 four dollar bills, worn out, have been
redeemed with specie since last report......   175   0
459 one dollar bills, rendered useless by
wear, have also been redeemed since last
report 114 15
The following bills have been redeemed at,
and received from the military chest at
Montreal, viz. :—

19,463 bills at 4 dollars...... £19,463   0
56,354 bills at 1 dollar 14,088 10   33,551 10

117 bills at 10 dollars	Of the new issue of		
137 " " 5 "	small bills rendered		
105 " " 3 "	useless by wear, or		
81 " " 2 "	otherwise, have been		
308 " " 1 "	redeemed between		
———	the 27th March and		
2,640 dollars	24th April, 1815...	660 0	£38,139 5

Balance of army bills remaining in circulation the 24th
April, 1815...... .... £1,211,857   0

To the Commissioners   .   (Signed) JAMES GREEN,
for fixing the rate of exchange,   Director.
&c. &c. &c.

Circulation of Army Bills.

ARMY BILL OFFICE,

22nd May, 1815.

ACCOUNT OF THE AMOUNT OF ARMY BILLS IN CIRCULATION.

Balance of army bills remaining in circulation the 24th
April, 1815... .... £1,211,857   0

DEDUCT :—

So much redeemed by bills of exchange on London
since the 24th April, 1815, viz. :—
In large bills. ... .£ 831   5
In small bills 2,932   5
                                          ———£3,763 10

150 four dollar bills, worn out, have been
redeemed with specie since last report...... 150   0
708 one dollar bills, rendered useless by wear,
have also been redeemed since last report... 177   0

64 bills at 10 dollars ⎫
58   "   " 5   "   ⎪   Of the new issue of
110 "   " 3   "   ⎪   small bills rendered
209 "   " 2   "   ⎪   useless by wear, or
619 "   " 1   "   ⎬   otherwise, have been
Affidavit   ⎪   redeemed between the
  before the   ⎪   24th April and 22nd
  Judges... 1   "   ⎪   May, 1815..... ...   574 10   £4,665   0
  ———   ⎪
2,298 dollars ⎭

Balance of army bills remaining in circulation the 22nd
May, 1815. ....£1,207,192   0

To the Commissioners   (Signed) JAMES GREEN,
for fixing the rate of exchange,   Director.
        &c.   &c.   &c.

Circulation of Army Bills.

ARMY BILL OFFICE,
19th June, 1815.

ACCOUNT OF THE AMOUNT OF ARMY BILLS IN CIRCULATION.

Balance of army bills remaining in circulation the 22nd
May, 1815.......... ....£1,207,192 0

DEDUCT :—

So much redeemed by bills of exchange on London
since the 22nd May, 1815, viz. :—
In large bills..................... ..... £13,512 10
Four dollar bills worn out have been re-
redeemed with specie since last report.....
One dollar bills rendered useless by wear
have also been redeemed since last report...

30 Bills at 10 dollars	
8 " " 5 "	
26 " " 3 "	Of the new issue of
79 " " 2 "	small bills rendered
18 " " 1 "	useless by wear, or
Affidavit	otherwise, have been
before the	redeemed between
Judges... "	the 22nd May and
———	19th June, 1815... 148 10 £13,661 0
594 dollars	

Balance of army bills remaining in circulation the 19th
June, 1815.. ....£1,193,531 0

To the Commissioners   (Signed) JAMES GREEN,
for fixing the rate of exchange,   Director.
&c.   &c.   &c.

E

Circulation of Army Bills.

ARMY BILL OFFICE.

11th September, 1815.

ACCOUNT OF THE AMOUNT OF ARMY BILLS IN CIRCULATION.

Balance of army bills remaining in circulation the 14th
August, 1815...... ....£ 628,792 15

DEDUCT : —

So much redeemed by bills of exchange on London
since the 14th August, 1815, viz. :—

In large bills............. ·£75,125	0	
In small bills.... 47,240	0	
	£122,365	0

976 four dollar bills, worn out, have been
redeemed with specie since last report.....   976   0
4294 one dollar bills, rendered useless by
wear, have also been redeemed since last
report. 1,073 10

—Bills at 10 dollars	Of the new issue of		
— " " 5 "	small bills rendered		
— " " 3 "	useless by wear, or		
— " " 2 "	otherwise, have been		
— " " 1 "	redeemed between		
Affidavits	the 14th August and		
before the	11th September,		
Judges.....6 "	1815 Affidavit	1 10	£124,416 0
6 dollars			

Balance of army bills remaining in circulation the 11th
September, 1815.............. ....£ 504,376 15

To the Commissioners   (Signed) JAMES GREEN,
for fixing the rate of exchange   Director.
     &c. &c. &c.

Circulation of Army Bills.

ARMY BILL OFFICE,
9th October, 1815.

ACCOUNT OF THE AMOUNT OF ARMY BILLS IN CIRCULATION.

Balance of army bills remaining in circulation the 11th
September, 1815.............. ....£504,376 15
No large or ten dollar bills issued since 11th
September, 1815.

DEDUCT :—

So much redeemed by bills of exchange on London since
the 11th September, 1815, viz.:—
In large bills.................£43,331   5
In small bills................. 25,649 0 £68,980 5

240 four dollar bills, worn out, have been
redeemed with specie since last report......   240 0
663 one dollar bills, rendered useless by
wear, have also been redeemed since last
report....... ....   165 15   69,386 0

Balance of army bills remaining in circulation the 9th
October, 1815........... ....£434,990 15

To the Commissioners   (Signed)   JAMES GREEN,
for fixing the rate of exchange,   Director.
&c. &c. &c.

Circulation of Army Bills.

ARMY BILL OFFICE,
6th November, 1815.

ACCOUNT OF THE AMOUNT OF ARMY BILLS IN CIRCULATION.

Balance of army bills remaining in circulation·the 9th
October, 1815.................. ....£434,990 15
No large or ten dollar bills since that date

DEDUCT :—

So much redeemed by bills of exchange on London since
the 9th October, 1815, viz.:—
In large bills.................£16,943 15
In small bills. 10,695 10
                          ——— £27,639 5
94 four dollar bills, worn out, have been
redeemed with specie since last report......   94 0
426 one dollar bills, rendered useless by
wear, have also.been redeemed since last
report.................. ....   106 10   27,839 15

Balance of army bills remaining in circulation the 6th
November, 1815....... ....£407,151 0

To the Commissioners   (Signed) JAMES GREEN,
for fixing the rate of exchange,   Director.
    &c. &c. &c.

General abstract of statements shewing the manner in which the sum of £88,962 10. currency, imprested to me by warrants from His Excellency Sir George Prevost, and His Excellency Sir Gordon Drummond, between the 11th October, 1814 and 24th August, 1815, has been appropriated.

A. Statement of one dollar bills redeemed between the 13th September, 1814, and 6th November, 1815 inclusive, your reports transmitted to the Commissary-General from time to time, in conformity to instructions from His Excellency Sir George Prevost, Governor-in-Chief and Commander of the forces............ ....£16,029 5

B. Statement of four dollar bills redeemed within the above period, and reported to the Commissary-General..... 14,381 0

C. Statement of bills of 10, 5, 3, 2 and 1 dollars, of the last emission, rendered useless by wear, or otherwise, which have been redeemed within the same period, and reported to the Commissary-General as above..... ... 8,879 0

D. Statement showing how the sum of £48,962 10. currency, has been appropriated, which I received for the purpose of exchanging small notes with bills bearing interest of 400, 100 and 50 dollars each. 48,962 10

E. Statement showing the number of counterfeit bills which were discovered in the military chest at Quebec and redeemed by me with specie, paid to John Hale, Esq., Deputy Paymaster-General, pursuant to the military Secretary's letter, dated Head Quarters, Montreal, 16th November, 1814........................ ...... 39 10

£88,291 5

Balance remaining in my hands on the 6th November, 1815, for the purpose of daily changing small notes of the above description............................. 617 5

£88,908 10

Errors excepted.   (Signed) JAMES GREEN,
    Army Bill Office,   .   Director.
    22nd Nov., 1815.

Circulation of Army Bills.

ARMY BILL OFFICE,
4th December, 1815.

ACCOUNT OF THE AMOUNT OF ARMY BILLS IN CIRCULATION.

Balance of army bills remaining in circulation the 6th
November, 1815..... ... .£407,151 0
No issue of large or ten dollar bills since that date

DEDUCT :—

So much redeemed by bills of exchange on London since
the 6th November, 1815, viz :—
In large bills..................·.£1,187 10
In small bills... .... 4,582 15 £5,770 5

So much redeemed by specie, commencing
the 24th November, 1815.
In large bills........ ... .£3,318 15
In small bills.... ,............... 801 15 £4,120 10

174 four dollar bills, worn out, have been redeemed with specie since last report......... 174 0
1231 one dollar bills, rendered useless by wear,
have also been redeemed since last report..... 307 15 £10,372 10

Balance of army bills remaining in circulation
the 4th December, 1815................ .... £396.778 10

To the Commissioners   (Signed) JAMES GREEN,
    for fixing the rate of exchange,   Director.
        &c. &c. &c.

MEMO.—Letter from James Green, Director, dated 18th December, 1815, asking for further warrant for £10,000 currency, to pay interest on army bills.

Report of Circulation, 1st January, 1816, gives balance in circulation 4th December, 1815, £396,778 0; from which deduct bills redeemed to 1st January, £65,281 15; leaving a balance in circulation 1st Jan., 1816, of £331,496 15.

Report of Circulation, 29th January, 1816, says, balance in circulation 1st January, 1816, £331,496 15; from which deduct bills redeemed to 29th January, 1816, £30,213; leaving a balance of army bills remaining in circulation the 29th January, 1816, of £301,283 15.

Report of Circulation, 26th February, 1816, says, balance in circulation 29th January, £301,283 15; deduct bills redeemed, £21,563 15; leaving a balance of £279,720 0.

Report of Circulation, 25th March, 1816, says, from balance 26th February, deduct in bills redeemed, £36,970 10; leaving balance of £242,749 10.

Report of Circulation, 22nd April, 1816, says, from balance 25th March, deduct in bills redeemed, £16,678; leaving a balance of £226,071 10.

Report of Circulation, 20th May, 1816, says, from balance in circulation 22nd April, 1816, deduct in bills redeemed, £28,096 15; leaving a balance of £197,974 15.

MEMO.—From a letter signed James Jackson, dated 3rd June, 1816, to Lt.-Col. Fulton, I see that the value of a silver shilling at that time was 25 coppers.

NOTE.—In a letter from Geo. Wood, Com.-Genl., dated 8th October, 1818, to Major Bowles, Mil. Secretary, he states that during the summer of 1818, the rate of exchange for public bills was at par, while private bills had uniformly been below par, from one to three per cent., the demand for public bills having been very large.

NOTE.—From a letter dated 9th December, 1818, I find that the rate at which the dollar was issued to the troops was 4s. 8d.

NOTE.—From a proclamation issued by His Grace Charles Duke of Richmond, Lennox and Aubigny, Commander of the forces in Canada and British North America, dated 17th December, 1818, I find that the date of closing the army bill office was enlarged to the 1st April, 1819.

NOTE.—Letter from James Green, Director, asking for continuance of army bill office to 1st August, 1820, as it had been accurately ascertained that there remained to the Crown a saving of *nine thousand pounds and upwards on bills lost or destroyed to that amount*, and he wished to have time to carry the affairs of that office to a satisfactory close, as was usual with other public offices similarly situated. (Date of letter, 19th May, 1819.)

Office continued to six months after 1st August, 1819, by sanction of War Department (Treasury Chambers).

MEMO.—Grand total of the number of army bills issued, viz.:—

Bills at 400 dollars each	....	5,500	....£550,000			
" " 100 "	"	....	34.605	... 865.150		
" " 50 "	"	....	63.914	... 798,925		
" " 25 "	"	. ...	92,726	... 579,537 10		
				—————£2,793,612 10		
" " 10 "	"	....	127,600	....£319,000		
" " 5 "	"	....	72,000	.. . 90,000		
" " 3 "	"	....	64,000	... 48,000		
" " 2 "	"	....	106,500	.... 53.250		
" " 1 "	"	....	165,000	 41,250	£551,500 0	
Bills redeemed with } specie only...... }	at 4 dollars 52,131		52,131			
	at 1 dollar. 179,000 ...		44,750		96,881 0	
		Total....			£3,441,993 10	

NOTE.—Army bill office is ordered to be continued to 1st August, 1820. Army bill office is ordered to be continued to 24th December, 1820. From a letter, dated Treasury Chambers, 23rd October, 1820, the army bill office was finally closed 24th December, 1820, Mr. Green paying into the hands of Commissary-General Wood the balance remaining in his hands to pay interest, namely, £819 13s. 7d. currency, at the rate of 5s. currency to the dollar.

From the 1st of January, 1815, to the 23rd November, when notice was given of the intention of the government to redeem the army bills in circulation, there is no official notice respecting the rate of exchange for bills on London at 30 days sight. Neither can I find any quotation in the newspapers of the day, save one in the Quebec Gazette of the 14th September, 1815, under the head of "money," which is as follows:

"For sale at par, for cash; a few government bills of £300 and £100 sterling, at thirty days on London. Apply to the Editor."

The pacification of Europe had effected a great change in the value of bills drawn on the treasury in London. As the demand for such bills appears to have been limited in Canada, resort was had to the Boston and New York markets. The following correspondence, however, shows that financial operations in the United States, for the purpose of procuring specie to meet the exigencies of the public service in Canada, were attended with no little difficulty. The Commissary-General writes to the Military Secretary as follows:

COMMISSARY-GENERAL'S OFFICE,
QUEBEC, 15th May, 1815.

SIR,

I have the honour to report to you, for the information of His Excellency the Lt.-General Commanding, that I have this day received letters from Dy. Asst. Comy.-General Wybault, dated New York, the 3rd inst., in which he states, on the subject of his mission, that exchange at that place is at 4 per cent. discount, and that as the banks to the southward of Massachusetts have not yet commenced paying out specie, it is at a premium of four p. cent. at New York, making a loss of 8 per cent. on negociation, and it appears there would be the same loss at Boston. Mr. Wybault regrets that he is directed to sell bills for specie, as that will betray the secret of his mission. The first bill he attempts to sell, and the knowledge that he has bills for sale, will at once reduce the price, as it will naturally be supposed he requires a very large sum ; besides, as there will be a premium on the specie, the discount on the bills, if paid for in specie, will appear much higher than the current rate, which, for obvious reasons, ought not to be the case ; under these circumstances, and considering our extreme distress for money, not having a thousand pounds in the Canadas, without a chance of being relieved by an importation from England to any great extent, in consequence of the reports we have lately received through the press of extraordinary events in Europe, I beg to submit to His Excellency whether Mr. Wybault should not be directed to procure specie for the government bills in his possession upon the best terms he can effect the negociation ; receiving in payment American bank notes and then exchanging them for specie, making the real exchange upon the bills, and charging the premium upon the specie in his account of disbursements, with expenses of transportation and other charges generally attending the transaction.   I trust you will be pleased to lay this letter before His Excellency, that I may be honoured with his commands as early as possible.

I have the honor to be, Sir,

Your most obedient humble servant,

To MAJOR O. FOSTER,   (Signed)   W. H. ROBINSON,
    Military Secretary.   Comy.-Genl.

[From Canadian Archives, Series C 331, page 98.]

COPY OF LETTER RE BRINGING SPECIE INTO COUNTRY.

HALIFAX, 9th June, 1815.

SIR,

Finding that Commissary-General Robinson had written to the Deputy Commissary-General here, representing the very pressing demand for specie in the Canadas, I have made every exertion to afford you a supply, which I could not have been able to do but by obtaining a loan rom the Naval Storekeeper ; with the assistance of which I have directed to be shipped on board H.M.S. Bulwark £30,000 con-signed to Mr. Robinson.

I think it right to apprise you of our poverty, that you may not place too much reliance on supplies from hence.' At the same time I shall always be willing to make every exertion to afford you all the aid in my power.

I have the honour to be, Sir,

Your most obedient humble servant,

(Signed) J. C. SHERBROOKE,

Lt.-General.

Those letters were written after the news of the escape of Napoleon from Elba had reached this side of the Atlantic. All Europe was astir with excitement over his escape ; and the consequent certainty of war had a depressing effect upon the rate of exchange. Bills on the Treasury were quoted at 12% discount. But Waterloo brought peace. Bills on London rose in value ; and the discount on 30 days . sight bills was reduced to 1½ to 2% in Boston, at which rate it stood in October 1815, and continued at from 2% to 3% discount, till the 17th of April, 1816, when a temporary increase in the rate occurred.

The quotations in New York for Bills on London were rather misleading. They were quoted at a premium of from 10 % to 12% ; but a correspondent in Halifax of the Quebec Gazette, enlightens the public on the subject. The letter is dated 7th October, 1815, and is headed Bills of Exchange. " By the late arrivals from New York, we observe that Exchange on England is quoted at a Premium of from 10 to 12%, which causes much more speculation in this place. A person, unacquainted with the mode of transacting business in New York, would naturally infer that specie of some kind was the equivalent, and at the quoted Premium ; but their insolvent Bank paper is the payment—which paper is at a discount of 14% for silver or gold, consequently Bills on England, which are nominally at 10 to 12% Premium, may be bought in New York by sending on hard coin at a discount."

The price of gold in England from January, 1816, to June 9th of the same year, did not average over £4. 1s. 6d. currency, the mint price as I have before stated being £3 17s. 10½d. per ounce ; and from June to January 1817, the average for currency was £3 19s. The Bank of England, however, did not resume specie payments till 1823 ; but the difference between the price of gold in the currency of the country, and the mint price per ounce, seldom exceeded 2s. 6d. during the last years, i.e. from 1817 to 1823.

A plentiful supply of specie appears to have reached the Treasury in Quebec at last ; for in November it was announced that the army bills would be redeemed in cash. The following is the announcement :—

PROCLAMATION.

On the 23rd November, 1815, by His Excellency Sir Gordon Drummond, Commanding His Majesty's Forces, and Administrator-in-Chief of the Governments of Upper and Lower Canada.

Whereas, heretofore, for the purposes of maintaining the means of circulation and answering the exigencies of the public service, His Excellency Sir George Prevost, Baronet, then Commanding His Majesty's Forces in British North America, did make and prepare a number of bills denominated army bills, and caused the same from time to time to be issued from the army bill office, established for that purpose at the City of Quebec, agreeably to the provisions of the several acts made for the purpose of facilitating the circulation of army bills: And whereas, in and by the said acts, it is, amongst other things, enacted, that all interest upon such army bills shall cease from and after the fourteenth day, next after the day on which the same, by any proclamation or other public requisition by the Commander of His Majesty's forces for the time being, shall be called in, to be redeemed in cash : I have, therefore, thought fit to issue this Proclamation, and hereby do signify and make known, to all whom it may concern, that all Army Bills heretofore issued, and at present in circulation, are called in, to be redeemed in cash, at the said Army Bill Office, in the said City of Quebec; and that all Interest upon such Bills as aforesaid, shall cease from and after the fourteenth day next after the date of these presents. Of all which the Officers of His Majesty's Government, and generally all to whom these presents shall come, or may in any wise concern, are hereby required to take notice and govern themselves accordingly.

On the 20th of December, 1815, His Excellency Sir Gordon Drummond called Parliament together for the Despatch of business; and in his Speech from the Throne, he alluded to the army bills as follows :—

"You have had the satisfaction of seeing that the Executive Government has completely redeemed its pledge to the Public, by calling in and paying in cash the army bills which were in circulation."

To which the House replies :—

"We have seen with great satisfaction, that the Executive Government has completely redeemed its pledge to the Public, by calling in and paying in Cash the Army Bills which were in circulation. A measure which exemplifies, in a most striking manner, the national good faith, and which will, we trust, facilitate similar arrangements hereafter, should the Public interests ever require a renewal of them."

At the Provincial Parliament held at Quebec on the 15th of January, 1817, the Fifteenth section of the original Act prohibiting the exportation of specie and bullion from the Province, for a period of five years from the 1st August, 1812, was repealed.

And it was provided that the Army Bill Office should be continued for a limited period beyond the 1st of August, 1817, for the purposes of calling in and cancelling and paying all Army Bills that might remain in circulation after the 1st of August ; and that it should be lawful for the Governor to issue his warrant for a sum not exceeding seven hundred and fifty pounds currency, for the payment of such officers in the Army Bill Office as it may be found necessary to continue in the service till the 1st of August, 1818, for the purposes aforesaid.

But the date of closing was enlarged to the 1st of April, 1819 ; and further to the 24th December, 1820, when the Army Bill Office was finally closed.

This ends my exposition of the Army Bill Act, by means of which the exigencies of the public service were provided for during the war of 1812, a war which was entered upon by the British with the greatest reluctance ; but which was forced upon them by the Americans, with the ostensible object of establishing the principle that the Flag covers the merchandise, and the right of search for seamen who have deserted is inadmissible ; but really, " to wrest from Great

Britain the Canadas, and, in conjunction with Napoleon, to extinguish its maritime power and Colonial Empire." *

I have now the pleasure of stating that I am indebted to Mr. George Bethune of the branch of the Quebec Bank in Ottawa, for important information on the subject of this paper, which he obtained in the Archives Bureau at Ottawa ; and to the kindness of Mr. Douglas Brymner of that office, in directing him to records relating to operations under the Act.

---

* Alison's History.

MONTREAL:
"WITNESS" PRINTING HOUSE

www.ingramcontent.com/pod-product-compliance
Lightning Source LLC
Chambersburg PA
CBHW021524270326
41930CB00008B/1085